SLEEPING WIT

SLEEPING WITH THE MYTH OF FEAR

*Awaken to the true beauty
and the true spirit of you*

JULIE ANNE HART

Copyright © 2014 Julie Anne Hart

All rights reserved

This book contains material protected under International and Federal Copyright Laws and Treaties. Any unauthorized reprint or use of this material is prohibited. No part of this book may be reproduced or transmitted in any form or by any means, electronic or mechanical, including photocopying, recording or by any information storage and retrieval system without express written permission from the author/publisher.

Bradley Hand, Cambria and Wingdings 2 fonts used with permission from Microsoft.

ISBN-13: 978-1500201470

ISBN-10: 1500201472

CONTENTS

Introduction vii

PART ONE: THE JOURNEY 1

   Chapter One The Journey 3

   Chapter Two The Healing Way 25

   Chapter Three The Making of Relations 35

PART TWO: EMPOWERMENT 53

   Chapter Four How To Set Yourself Free And Dance With Life 55

   Chapter Five Taking The Leap Into Your Unlimited Potential 75

PART THREE: LEADERSHIP 87

   Chapter Six Big Heart, Big Purpose, Big Power 89

   Chapter Seven Abundance 99

About The Author 113

Index 114

INTRODUCTION

Sleeping With The Myth Of Fear

I have written this book to share with you part of my life experiences, coupled with some of the experiences of the clients I know and teach.

I have set up this book to guide you through a process, just as I would if you came to me as a private client or attended one of my retreats. My sincere wish for you is that, by the time you have finished reading and completed the exercises laid out in this book, you will have begun to change your life and acknowledge the truth of who you are.

It is my wish for you that you end the cycle of what I call 'sleeping with the myth of fear', feeling afraid to be everything and do everything that you have the potential for. I want you to wake up to the beauty of you, to your creativity on all levels. I want you to open your heart and acknowledge your truth - leaving behind a mindset that has kept you questioning and even unaware of your full potential.

I want to take you on a journey like never before. You are about to step onto a rollercoaster ride of emotions. The ride will wow you, change and shape you in ways you cannot yet imagine.

Over years of my own personal, professional, and spiritual development, I can now see the truth of myself. I'm a spiritually-gifted individual with a big heart and a big purpose and big power. Spiritual, creative power. I see the same gifts within my clients and within my work. I see the same pattern happening over and over again.

You do not need to fear failure, or fear that you are 'lesser than' or 'not enough'. The truth is you fear YOU. You fear the truth of who you are, pure divine love. You FEAR your creative spirit, you fear your spiritual power, you fear your potential, you fear yourself - all unique, all powerful, all creative, all mind-blowingly awesome.

You fear *you* so much that you have to talk down, diminish, and discard yourself through the power of what you have created. Your experiences will have mirrored your false belief system. Your false belief system served you as it protected you from looking into your unlimited creative potential.

ഌCര

Sleeping with the myth of fear will have kept you safe from having to face what you can do and be and create. It's a painful and sad place to stay, where life becomes a mindset of "I am not ....".

Your false beliefs have served you as they kept you low in true self-belief. It's your time to take responsibility.

Introduction

Waking up means firstly taking responsibility to see the truth of who you are and then to take responsibility for your past as a creator. It means understanding that your past has benefitted you, however painful it has been. When you understand you have been living asleep with myth of fear you awaken to love, abundance, and success. This is your birthright as a spiritual being having a human experience.

Waking up to the truth of ***you*** enables your world to change. You allow in only what you desire to experience in life. You walk a path of beauty and leave a trail of beauty for others to follow. Your opportunities become unlimited. Life becomes blissful as you move into creating the life you love to live in harmony and oneness with a growing purpose, spiritual power, and the true art of prosperity.

PART ONE

THE JOURNEY

THE JOURNEY
Why You Create What You Don't Want & How To Transform It

ೋರ೪

Welcome to your journey. The road to transformation is in always seeking your own truth and then stretching your concept to become it.

My Myth Of Fear

HOW CAN WE EVER TELL OURSELVES WE ARE ANYTHING LESS THAN BEAUTIFUL?

Taking responsibility as an infinite creator of my experiences, I have asked myself **why** I have created what I have in my life.

As I drop the blame and shame, I can clear the fog and see. As I remove the smoke screen that has clouded my vision and step out into a new reality, I can thank the fog and the smoke for keeping me safe. I can thank it but no longer want its services. As I wake up to a new revolution and a profound realisation, I cry for the little girl who couldn't see and the woman who had to hide and who refused to see.

Maybe you too are not living the life you want or being the person you know you can be. There is something inside that is hidden, that has been quietened or suppressed over decades until you have almost forgotten it is there. This is what I call the *Myth of Fear*.

I have hidden. I have denied. I have diminished my creative potential. I have minimised my spiritual power. I have felt like a failure and a fraud to my purpose - which is to make a difference on this planet. I have been asleep with the big myth. The myth gripped my mind and my heart.

That myth is the enemy.

It's ***fear***.

Sometimes you can spot it but most of the time it is unseen, deeply rooted in your psyche. You are asleep, unconscious to its presence and purpose.

We are born perfect, whole, and complete in our uniqueness and individuality. There is unbearable sadness to see the playfulness of a child enjoying the planet, learning, exploring, and seeking the adventure of life, only to begin the process of accepting little seeds of doubt, of inadequacy, of not being enough slowly taking away - bit by bit - all that is perfect.

You can take into consideration social, cultural, and environmental programming but there is so much more than these factors at play. There is so much more that you do not acknowledge. There is so much more potential to you that you fear to 'see' your truth.

As I look back upon my childhood, I cannot find one memory of feeling good about myself. I never felt accepted or good enough - from my earliest school memory to my home experiences. I cannot remember a positive statement or a kind word being spoken.

At school, I acknowledged what I could not do and this was reinforced by peers and teachers. I had a strong and vivid imagination but I struggled to write as I am dyslexic. It was never diagnosed.

I struggled with my identity and never felt I fitted in anywhere. The expectations of others diminished my sense of self and I began the process of pleasing everyone *else* so I could be accepted. In my shame, I blocked the creativity and turned my back on the beauty of the dreamer inside me.

My relationship with my parents was co-dependent.

It is hard to describe my childhood. On one level I had a warm, clean, and well provided-for home – but there was a price to pay. That price was criticism and control. I never felt good enough for my father. He always wanted more from me in terms of achievement and my mother told me I was ungrateful to want anything. What a bag of confusion I was.

Every relationship I experienced formed its own level of control and abuse. My worth and self esteem were, and have been for most of my life, rock bottom.

So if I – and you - am an infinite creator, why would I have **created** something so painful? Why would I think the way I did about myself?

I was frightened, I was scared, and I feared but what did I fear exactly? That I was not good enough? No I feared my **truth**.

> I DARE NOT SEE THE TRUTH
> FOR WHO AM I TO BE TALENTED, GIFTED,
> AND A POWERFUL CREATOR?
> WHO AM I NOT TO BE?

I was asleep with the **myth** of **fear**, unconscious to my beliefs. I gave away my power and potential, just handed it over. I surrendered it and released it to be controlled, diminished, and abused.

My inner truth was too much to handle. I created a smoke screen of illusion so I could stay safe in the control of others who didn't want me to progress because they feared my progression too.

Safe staying out of my true identify – because I feared it. Why? Because I am a spiritually and creatively gifted person who [unconsciously] didn't want to be **seen**.

Safe not to see my beauty, gifts, and talents or the gentle sensitive spirit I am. It was too much to acknowledge.

In my working career I always came up with some reason why I shouldn't go for a promotion or a higher position, mostly with an excuse that the game was too political or I didn't like the management's philosophy. But this was not the truth, just another smoke screen created from the myth of fear.

In my relationships I was extremely guarded. I had many friends but seldom allowed people to get close. I coupled this with the excuse that I didn't have the time. And so what I continued to experience were the same situations over and over again, continually creating a lack in my life on all levels: personal, professional, financial, emotional, and spiritual.

In this book I am going to walk you through a process that will take you from sleeping with your myth, to an awakening and a transformation that will change the way you feel about yourself and your life.

My Awakening

OPEN YOUR HEART AND EXPERIENCE

THE MIRACLE OF YOU.

In the summer of 2000 I experienced an emotional breakdown. I didn't know it at the time, but it was going to be the breakthrough to reveal what was really inside – my inner truth.

I was in the midst of what I thought was some kind of breakdown. I thought it was stress at work, or health problems but these were just manifestations of a bigger shift.

Not knowing where to turn, I booked myself a spiritual healing session with a friend and colleague. I had no idea what to expect, but what happened in that 60-minute session dramatically changed something in my mind, body, and spirit. Something that could not be undone.

I experienced a deep spiritual awakening that gave me the gift of using my sixth sense of vision, hearing, feeling, knowing, and receiving information and guidance on a spiritual level. My connection to those in the spirit world started to open up.

I thought I'd simply gone mad.

I saw angels and communicated with spirits. I became aware of who was guiding and assisting me. I connected with the angelic realms for healing and enlightenment. I spoke to my ancestors and loved ones in the spirit world.

I was shocked and amazed.

This kind of experience is a pure connection to pure love. That is what spirituality is.

It was so emotional to be touched by such a powerful, loving presence and energy. I cried for a week. I cried each time I connected to this energy. I cried because this kind of totally accepting and unconditionally loving presence was alien to me.

My spiritual wakening opened up a new reality, a new consciousness of existence. It was more than what had been my reality, it was now so much more.

I owe my spiritual awakening to Susan Macdonald, one awesomely powerful woman. A healer, therapist, counsellor, and teacher, Sue is definitely a medicine woman in her own right. Her gifts are beyond words. Her presence is one of love and kindness. My sister, teacher, and friend, I am blessed that our paths crossed.

I began to ask myself questions about who I was and why I felt the way I did. Where does that pure unconditioned beauty disappear to?

The Journey

My personal and spiritual development started right there on 5th June 2000, 34 years after my birth. I allowed myself to come out and begin to heal the myth I had created, although to some degree I was still asleep with the myth of fear.

Now I was beginning to return to my pure essence, it blew my mind. It created fear like never before but I handled it as I made friends with my fear.

※

In the sections that follow I want to take you on my journey and show you how you too can walk the path that I have. To step into the power that is you and live with the freedom that is possible for you.

> YOUR AUTHENTIC POWER IS ALL ENCOMPASSING LOVE. IT HOLDS NO BOUNDARIES OR LIMITATIONS IN ITS CAPACITY AND CAPABILITY TO LOVE AND TO CREATE TOTAL BEAUTY IN ALL YOUR EXPERIENCES.

Your authentic power is powerful - that's why you fear it.

My life experiences, that had once been unconsciously comfortable in confusion and inner conflict, became consciously unacceptable. I had a new sense of desire to do more, to be more, to achieve more in a heart-centred way. I was waking up to my truth and it's been a journey of acknowledging me, honouring me, respecting me, and loving myself. It's been a journey to seeing, knowing, and feeling my worth, coupled with total acceptance of who I am.

Now I can say yes to living and creating with the life I love. I have had to do the work, make the commitment and face my fear, but it's been an amazing journey to love and I want to share some of it with you so you can have the same choice.

How The Myth Of Fear Paralyses Your Potential

FEAR VERSUS LOVE

It is safer and less fearful to deny your magnificence than it is to lovingly accept and embrace it.

When your mind merges with the myth of fear you are in total denial of who you are and the potential that you hold. You will hold tightly onto a false belief system that will create confusion and inner conflict. You will believe you are not worthy, deserving or lovable. You will not be able to receive the fruits of this planet in all its abundance.

You *fear* love.

Fear has served you and kept your true self and potential safe, hidden, and unseen with a mindful of reasons, thoughts, and feelings that do not allow you to see the beauty or power of the self.

Fear will diminish your unique creative essence and safeguard you through the prevention of embracing the truth of who you are.

Fear does not exist only in the myth of your mind. Fear is your resistance to opening up to positive, loving, creativity energy.

Take a moment now to reflect on your past and present life experiences. What beliefs did or do you hold? How do you relate these experiences to how you feel about yourself? Check out where you are right now.

If your thoughts and feeling about you are loving and positive you are waking up to your truth. If they are not then you are still sleeping with the myth of fear.

I define love as universal energy that creates everything: our planet, the stars, the sun, the seasons, and each new day. The same energy that created all things is the same energy that runs through you. It is divine source energy.

The spirit of all matter starts as energy. Love is a creative stream of loving, life-force energy that, when accessed, will enable you to have unlimited potential and opportunities.

LOVE IS A POWERFUL THING THAT MOVES MOUNTAINS AND BIRTHS MIRACLES.

You are divine love, a spiritual being in human form. Your spirit is unconditional love, all powerful, all creative, all healing, all knowing. It is eternal. Love is such an overwhelming, powerfully beautiful force you will and do fear it.

The River Of Life

CLEANSE, HEAL, AND EMPOWER TO FLOW WITH LIFE IN HAPPINESS, JOY, AND HARMONY.

Your beliefs, thoughts, and feelings carry a vibration - an energetic life-force frequency that creates an outcome. Your beliefs are what you have been experiencing.

There are two streams of life-force energy. One is fear-based and feeds your myth; the other is positive, loving energy. When you are asleep with the myth of fear you block off the stream of loving energy that limits your potential on all levels.

Moving into the flow of positive, loving energy where your creative potential is unlimited requires you to drop the myth of fear and open your heart to love all that life has to give to you and to the loving presence of which you are.

To keep in the stream of positive creative energy you have to move through three stages: healing, empowerment, and leadership. You are about to be taken through this process.

This is your journey it's a gift.

Divine love is universal energy that creates your heart's desire into your physical reality. Which stream do you choose to connect to? The choice is yours.

Shaking Off The Myth Of Fear

> FREEDOM IS YOUR BIRTHRIGHT!
> WHEN YOU ARE FREE THERE IS NO ROOM
> FOR FEAR. IT HAS NO POWER OVER YOU.

Fear does not exist, only in the myth of your mind. It is the mind you must make friends with and constantly communicate lovingly to. Your myth of fear will feed your doubt, worry, and anxiety and make sure you keep away from having any trust or faith in your true essence.

I have worked with clients who are remarkably talented and spiritually powerful healers, coaches, and mentors.

There is a common theme that runs through all their stories. That theme is one of co-dependent relationships, self abuse, and negative self beliefs about themselves, their skills, and talents. I have noticed and studied very creative and spiritually-talented people diminish their power and potential through the power of self denial.

This is just fear of the truth of what they hold. They sleep with this myth until the myth becomes too painful to continue believing in. This is the point of transition and awakening.

Your fear will tell you a million reasons why you cannot or should not do a certain thing. It will tell you whatever it needs to tell you to keep you where you have always kept yourself,. Your fear has, until now, been laid so deeply-rooted in your unconscious that you have not been aware of its presence.

Your fear will speak through your experiences. If you have not allowed yourself to be happy and creative, and have the life your want, it is because you fear it. If you have not allowed yourself to be your potential or receive your prosperity, it is because you fear it.

※

On a soul level, you know you are not what you think but your head and your heart are in conflict. It is so overwhelming to acknowledge yourself as special, unique, and perfect in imperfection just as you are. It is too emotional to acknowledge all your talents and gifts.

The life-force energy on our planet has been predominately fear-based and humankind has feared the spiritual power within the human being, which has compound your fear of your amazing spirit.

Your myth of fear was only trying to do its best for you to keep you safe, hidden, and playing small. You are the creator of all your experiences. In the myth of fear, your beliefs aided and assisted you as you created painful experiences that purposely kept you out of seeing the truth of who you are.

Releasing the myth of fear means making friends with your fear and entering into positive, truthful communication. The more you communicate with the voice of fear in your head, the more you will reprogram your new beliefs.

I want you to pay less attention to your head and listen to your heart. What message is your heart giving you? What do you desire to achieve or create? What is your passion? What is your purpose? Allow yourself to start and feel excited about life. It's all there for you.

Releasing the myth of fear will take commitment, determination, and persistence in trusting in yourself and having faith in yourself to follow your dream and live it.

Waking Up To Your Truth

THE MOMENT OF ENLIGHTENMENT,

THE BIRTH OF MIRACLES.

Waking up is a gift. It will show you what you do not want, what you do want, and what you need to heal, empower, and transform to achieve your desired outcome. Your past experiences are the gift that gave you this awareness. Without the experience you could never have had the wisdom to know the self with such clarity.

You know you are waking up when what you have been experiencing is no longer wanted. You will feel the calling to do more and be more and the primary gains of your false belief system will no longer be required by you. You will not want to experience anything less than your heart desires. You will desire to experience good things in your life. You will want to feel good in yourself. You will want to fulfil your potential and purpose on the planet.

You are waking up to love. You will intuitively know that what you think is not real, it's not you. You will want to find the true spirit of you and let it out and let love in.

You incarnated into life with a purpose, with a mission to complete and achieve. It starts with you discovering this information.

Your past has no power over you unless you allow it to. The past does not affect your future. You can change your past, shape your present, and transform your future just by acknowledging the truth in all things.

You Are Not Your Story

END THE DRAMA. IT SERVES YOU NOT.

Waking up is a process of discovery and transformation.

You are not a victim, you are not your past, you are not your story. You are a unique and powerful individual. Telling your story from a stance of "Poor me" will not serve the new you. If you are going to speak or think about your past, tell it from a place of empowerment of enlightenment, of seeking and of understanding who you are.

Do you find yourself making statements like, "My mother didn't love me. She wanted me to be blonde, or prettier."? I don't feel lovable. My father told me I needed to achieve more. I never did, I felt like a failure.

You are experiencing your myth of fear what you are creating is total denial of your magnificence, that is really what you don't want to see!

The Journey

I want you to say these words out loud:
- I am are a co-creator.
- I have written my own play.
- I invited the players in.
- I chose these experiences. Has it served me to do so?
- My story is one of power and purpose that benefits myself and others.
- As I wake up to my truth, I can change my script and the players in it.
- It's my show.
- I have experienced everything in life for a reason. The past is over and that reason is no longer needed.
- I am not my story.

Now say them again, this time with more feeling.

Change Your Perception

WHY MOVING OUT OF YOUR OWN WAY IS VITAL.

The way you think, feel, and speak about your life experiences will determine how you view yourself. It's time to stop saying "I am not..." or "I didn't get it right..."

I want you to change the way you perceive your past and yourself. This is the first step to freeing yourself from your myth of fear.

View your life experiences as positive, see only the good.

Allow your past experiences to be inspirational to you so you can have emotional freedom and set yourself free of the shackles of your mind. Honour and respect your qualities, strength, and courage.

There are no mistakes in life, only lessons in love. Instead of regretting past experiences, let your past teach you wisdom, let it make the present be your gift.

Your past experiences are not you! Yes, you have experienced what you have but they do not form your character or personality. Your uniqueness and authenticity is based on what you choose it to be and is not the total sum of your experiences.

As you drop the myth of your fear, see all past events as miracles that shaped you into finding your truth. Your past has now brought you to the power of the present moment.

Positive appreciation of the past will give to you so much that the gift will be invaluable to you and you will begin to think and feel so differently that a whole new world of opportunities will naturally open up to you.

> IT MATTERS NOT WHAT YOU HAVE EXPERIENCED. WHAT IS IMPORTANT IS WHERE YOU ARE HEADING.

Every experience has a purpose and is powerful. Every experience you have or have had can be used in a way that serves your highest good.

Move your present perception to shape the reality you now desire to experience and live. Your perception will affect your emotional health and wellness. It will affect your ability to be happy, whole, and free. You can choose to change your perception in any given moment.

Take "I can't do it" out of your language. "I can't" means you do not want to. It means you're still wanting to sleep with the myth of fear. Whenever you feel stuck, choose to do something new or look at something in a new way.

How To Grow Roses And Not Weeds

LIFE IS YOUR GARDEN.

IT IS UP TO YOU WHAT YOU PLANT.

It is like weeding a garden, you have to keep tending it and pulling out the weeds. The mind is the same. When you are awake you do have conscious choice about what you believe.

Feed yourself the truth. It's easy – remember, you have been feeding yourself the myth of fear for years. You had no problem doing that so you will not have a problem retraining and reprogramming your myth of fear as you attune it to believe your truth.

Weave Your Own Web Of Desire

> PASSION IS THE FIRE ENERGY
> THAT RUNS THROUGH YOUR BLOOD.
> IT IS CALLING YOU TO CREATE.

Are you weaving or are you caught up in the cobwebs of your past creation? You will, at times, find yourself believing, thinking, feeling, and doing the old worn-out, familiar behaviour. It's ok, you have spotted it just in time before you get caught in your own web.

Weave and keep weaving your heart-centred passion, regardless of what it takes, focusing on what your heart desires only. As I look at the spider weaving the web of creation, it is so delicately-woven. The spider never thought that she couldn't do it, she just went ahead and wove her beauty for the world to see and it delivered her exactly what she desired to receive.

How To Take The Journey With Ease And Self Care

> BE KIND. BE COMPASSIONATE.
> BE YOUR OWN HEALER.

Transformation takes time. You will swing back and forth on this emotional rollercoaster ride.

You are aware that your myth of fear will tell you false messages - you know you will have to speak lovingly to these messages. You understand that the more you

The Journey

reinforce the truth of who you are, the more you move away from your myth of fear.

There is a new world of opportunities now opening up to you. You are an unlimited creator with unlimited potential.

You are awake to experiencing this, how wonderful! It's like you have been hiding behind a curtain just peeking around it to see what's there. Now you can come out once and for all.

You can do this, you can free yourself from your myth of fear. You will need to be very awake to what you are creating. As you complete the healing work in chapters two and three, make a commitment to be loving and kind to yourself. Make your journey easy and enjoyable with lots of self-care. Then you will naturally move on to the self-empowerment stage.

As you continue to walk your journey, you will take the transformation to leading in all areas of your life. This is your time to live the life you love. Congratulations - you have just won the lottery! Life in all its bliss awaits you.

Empowered leadership in all areas of your life means you allowing yourself to open your heart and become your innermost desire.

Drop the drama of the mind and if you cannot think good thoughts then think nothing. Placing your mind into neutral so you can listen to your heart, your inner wisdom, the intuitive part of you that holds the answers, will give you peace, harmony, and freedom from the familiar programme that you have had running until now.

Discovering your true identity and spirit is blissful. Now you can move into a better feeling place. What needs to happen next is your ability to move beyond forgiveness in total acceptance of yourself, your experiences, and everyone who has played a part in your life.

Exercise

> DISCOVER THE SPIRIT OF YOU.
> ACKNOWLEDGE THE TRUTH OF
> WHO YOU ARE.

Take some time for yourself in a space where you will not be disturbed, a space that you feel good spending time in, a space that is clean and tidy for you to relax in.

- ➢ Sitting comfortably, relax and take several deep breaths in and out.
- ➢ Close your eyes and give yourself praise and approval. Say good things to yourself.
- ➢ Honour and respect yourself and love yourself more by acknowledging you are free from blame, shame, worry, doubt, and criticism. Allow only the good thoughts to come into your mind.
- ➢ Make a commitment to see the beauty and amazingness in yourself. Acknowledge the powerful person you are. Acknowledge your skills and abilities.
- ➢ Determine to be loving and kind.

- Keep a journal to monitor your beliefs, thoughts, and feelings.
- Commit to a regular writing habit – once a day if you can. Try this for a week at least.

Affirmation Work For Letting Go

⇨ New wisdom is now coming my way. I show my appreciation for these new understandings that allow me to grow. I stand in appreciation for my life lessons for they have given to me a sense of self that will serve me for the rest of my life. The gift of wisdom is in your heart and remains alive as long as you honour it as a blessing.

THE HEALING WAY
How The Power Of Acceptance Heals, Empowers And Transforms

~~~~~~

For most of my life I had played the 'martyr', leading my life by meeting others' needs and expectations, with a need to be accepted and approved of. If I made choices for myself without that approval, I felt extremely guilty and shameful.

All of my life I felt that I needed to make amends for what I had got wrong, for marrying the wrong guy, for doing the wrong job, for looking, thinking, and feeling the wrong way. The list went on and on.

Until one day I woke up to: "This is my life and I am OK to think, feel, and choose."

My spirit has always been strong and free but so squashed by the demands and expectations of others, of course this had been unconsciously comfortable up until this point of transition in my life.

I decided to leave a professional career and open a small holistic shop in the heart of the Peak District. My friends and some family members where so shocked. "But what about your salary or pension or income" or, even worse, "You will lose your professional stature".

My father was so disapproving as I developed my spiritual awareness and therapeutic skills that he stopped acknowledging this side to me completely. All he wanted me to do was go back to work and live the mainstream way as a 9 to 5 hamster in a wheel to pay my mortgage, have 2 weeks holidays, save for a pension, fill my ISA each year, and invest in a few stocks and shares.

I have had this message all my life and it was so boring. I was not going to waste any more time fulfilling the expectations of others. I did it. I jumped into a new way of thinking, feeling, and doing and I held the faith and trust both in myself and in the universe to support me.

I had at this point started the journey of acceptance of myself, of who I was and what my beliefs were, regardless of others' fears, thoughts, and opinions. It was a powerful, fearful, magical, and exciting time. So many emotions all rolled into one.

Accepting myself and starting the coming out process of saying, "This is me and I am now beginning to like and love myself devoid of the need for others," is a magical experience and allowed me the freedom of choice.

The only relationship you truly have is the one with the self and you will need the power of acceptance to set you free it set me free moving me beyond forgiveness and into peace, as I accepted all my life experiences as a gift I felt the healing and freedom from anger resentment and pain.

※

I have cried buckets, screamed, shouted, and hated a few people along my way. I let it all go with the healing power of acceptance. It was total **bliss** not to be carrying emotions that did not serve me.

Your emotions are gifts. They all carry a message but it's up to you to decide to only carry loving messages and release painful ones.

My relationship with my father was very close. He was my inspiration. Although he has passed I know he still does want the best for me. However, his words always felt critical as I was growing up and I felt like I was never enough for him. I needed his acceptance.

He guided me into careers that were never in alignment with who I was. They where what he wanted me to be. As soon as I moved into accepting **me**, it had enormous healing power. As I healed through the power of acceptance, I allowed others to accept the true me - or not, it was as simple as that!

I was blessed that, for the final years of my father's life, he got to know the true me and he did accept my spiritual gifts and support my chosen path. Our relationship grow in closeness and understanding through the power of acceptance.

Here is the most powerful thing that acceptance brings - it catapulted me into my potential through the power of unconditional love. My father gave me his acceptance of who I was because I gave myself acceptance to be me for the first time in my life.

It felt awe-inspiringly powerful and loving. It gave me and my father a chance to get to know each other in our uniqueness. Acceptance is healing, empowering, and transformational. It moves you beyond forgiveness and into the loving beauty of insight and inner knowing.

The Purpose and Power of Acceptance

To live the life you love to its fullest potential without the barriers of fear stopping you, you will need to accept yourself on all levels and then stretch your concept of who you are.

What Is Acceptance?

Definitions of ACCEPTANCE:

1. The act or **process** of **accepting** a state of being **accepted**.
2. A **favourable reception**.
3. An **approval** of or **belief** in something powerful.

Acceptance is unconditional love. Acceptance is to 'see' the truth in a situation to gain insight and to open your heart to a higher belief system that will move your beyond forgiveness and into the freedom of understanding where you hold the powerful emotion of love.

Why Is Acceptance Healing?

The definition of HEALING:

To restore to health or soundness; to cure.

Definition of CURE:

1. To set **right**; **repair**: healed the **rift** between us.
2. To **restore** (a person) to **spiritual wholeness**.
3. To become **whole** and sound; return to **health**.

Acceptance of the self will restore your health and well-being. It will bridge the gap between your head and your heart so they match up and support your truth. Acceptance births insight, it restores wholeness between people and life experiences. Acceptance allows you to release past pain and return to wholeness through releasing anger and resentment and toxic emotions that no longer serve you.

Through the power and purpose of acceptance you will come to know and love the self. It is the only way you can be who you are. Without acceptance you are in denial of your potential and purpose on the planet. Without acceptance you will not be able to release beliefs of the self that no longer serve you. They are old and worn out and cannot be carried into the power of the present moment. They will block your future potential.

Acceptance brings you freedom of choice and opens your heart to endless loving opportunities.

The Rewards Of Acceptance

How to take responsibility in a loving kind way.

Let's look at the healing power of acceptance. Acceptance allows you to move beyond forgiveness. It is unconditional Divine love in its purist form. Acceptance is the way you can move into a better feeling place. Acceptance brings you inner peace and unconditional love - and love is the creative force.

Whatever your experiences have been up to this point in your life, you where instrumental in the creation of them and they would have served you in a way that suited you.

Your parents, family, friends, and colleagues are all players in your script. Regardless of what you have experienced or how you feel about people, when you surrender and release the past and move into acceptance, you take a healing transformation that moves you into your loving powerful essence.

INSPIRATION: WHAT IT WILL TAKE TO CHANGE

It will take strength, courage, and healing to accept yourself and others and all your experiences. You will have to release all negative emotions that are critical, judgmental, blaming, or shaming.

REWARD: WHY IT'S ESSENTIAL

Acceptance is a vital principle in your leadership creation and the first step to your healing journey. Acceptance is a loving ownership of the self, and a philosophy to allow others to be who they are. Acceptance places you in an emotional vibration and frequency to attract more Health, Wealth and Prosperity.

What You Will Feel At The End Of This Stage

As you commence the process of moving into acceptance you will feel a freedom so powerful it will naturally inspire you to move into your potential. As you accept yourself you will find it easier to accept your past and all who played a part in it.

Taking the leap truly in your power, opening your heart to more love, success, and abundance requires you to be a vibrational match for what is around you. Unconditional acceptance of all things is that match.

What It Means/Does Not Mean

Acceptance does not mean tolerance. If you are tolerating something or someone then you're not free. There is still a feeling of resentment, of a lack of power. Tolerance means you are not allowing yourself to receive your heart's desire. When you 'accept' you are opening yourself to forgiveness and to generosity.

I want you to accept your life experiences, but to tolerate nothing that you do not want to have in your life. Tolerance keeps you trapped. Acceptance allows healing.

Exercise

How to move into The Healing Power of Unconditional Acceptance

This can be an emotional exercise so it's important to take good loving care of yourself. Ask a friend for support. Do not judge or criticise how you feel - just accept what is true for you – there is no judgement, only love.

- Create a clean and tidy environment to relax in where you will not be disturbed.
- Reflect and write down the experiences you have had that have hurt you or caused you pain.
- Write down the emotions you feel about yourself. Be honest, do not hold back.
- Write down the emotions you feel for the people that have been in your life.
- Allow whatever emotions to rise to the surface and take several deep breaths in and out until the feeling eases and releases.
- Have a willingness to release yourself from any negative thoughts and feelings you have for yourself and others.
- Tell yourself you love and accept all parts of you and all your experiences in life.

> Without any questioning, just accept all of your experiences: people, places, situations. Allow your life to just be.

> Now give thanks to all the situations for they have brought you to this powerful point in your life where you are not stepping up into more.

> Take a deep breath in and out as this is a huge request but the rewards will be profound for you.

Your healing journey is accelerated through the power of acceptance, with increased amounts of trust and faith the very energy that moves mountains

Repeat this exercise whenever you feel out of alignment with unconditional acceptance.

> *"Understanding is the first step to acceptance, and only with acceptance can there be recovery."*
>
> J.K. Rowling
> *Harry Potter and the Goblet of Fire*

Affirmation Work

⇗ I now accept all past experiences. I am free.

THE MAKING OF RELATIONS
A heart-to-heart connection with another that can only be gained through understanding and acceptance

ಸಿಂಲ್

The more insight and acceptance you have with heartfelt compassion for all your relationships, the more you will open up to feeling and receiving more love, more success, and more abundance.

My healing journey began with me beginning the journey of self-acceptance and then moving deeper into self love.

It was, at first, a difficult process as I had to own and feel what I had thought about myself for most of my life. There had been little love in terms of a loving partner and my relationship with my parents had remained co–dependent.

As I healed, I offered a chance for my family and loved ones to heal too. As I moved out of my career and into doing the work I felt passionate about, my relationships with the people in my life had to move to a healthier connection.

As I moved to a new stage in my life, it transformed all my relationships in different ways. When you take the healing journey, those around you have the chance to heal and step up with you – or it becomes too much for them to be in healthy positive energy.

I had to acknowledge that I had to let some friends go. I had to heal, accept, and gain insight into my relationship with my parents and others. As I did this my relationship with my mother and father took a total catalytic transformation for us all that set us free to be the true spiritual essences that we are.

As we move together from acceptance to healing, I want to show you how powerful it can be to give yourself the gift of healing and how healing is necessary to empowerment. To step into your leadership you must first go on your own healing journey. Let me introduce you to what that journey can be for you in this chapter.

The Insight To Understand

INSIGHT GRACES YOU

WITH THE GIFT OF UNDERSTANDING.

My mother was a worrier and she never ever saw the truth of herself. She was a very gifted person with a very big heart but she totally feared her skills and talents.

My mother had been ill since being 45 years old, she was paralyzed with arthritis. Fear cripples you and hers did. My mother's fear got transferred on to me. She was the original Cinderella. She never allowed herself to go to the ball and she expected me to do the same.

As I moved out of the program that she had parented, one of being the martyr to others' needs, I faced so much guilt and shame. Who was I to have a choice and live? The truth was, who was I not to?!

Guilt and shame are often the primary emotions to the barriers to your purpose, potential, and prosperity. The truth is there is no guilt or shame, it does not exist, only in the myth of fear. Fear creates your mind myth. I had created my myth of fear-based emotions so I could remain safe unseen and unloved because I feared who I was and I feared love.

My mother resisted my move of career and really struggled with it. "You will not survive and you are too far away," she would say. My mother never wanted any of her family to move on. For years, everything had to stay the same with no change. It was the only way she could feel safe. I would speak with her and after a short while I would find myself shaking in my shoes as the energy of fear surrounded us. Our talks were seldom a positive experience.

My mother passed away 3 months after I made my big career move. She did visit, but only once.

I do feel by giving myself loving permission to live the life I loved, I gave her permission to choose what she wanted to experience in her life for the first time ever!

My mother decided it was time to move on to the next phrase in her life. She passed away the same way she lived her life - very quietly. I can hear her saying, "I will not be any trouble." Having seen all her family, she just slipped away. It was a total shock but I knew she had made a decision to go. We both now had new paths to walk.

Reach Out In Understanding

> SEEING THE TRUTH IN YOURSELF AND IN ANOTHER PERSON AND UNDERSTANDING THEIR JOURNEY TOTALLY TRANSFORMS YOUR INNERMOST FEELINGS.

My mother and I were unable to have a really well-connected, loving relationship even though we loved each other.

There was too much baggage that got in our way. She was fearful of life and resentful of not living the life she had wanted to. It was too overwhelmingly painful for her to see me giving that to myself so it was safer all round for her to martyr us both.

As I healed, it broke the cycle of control and fear but, sadly, she passed away before we got chance to heal our relationship in physical form.

I feel privileged to be blessed with the gift of being able to connect and communicate with the spirit world and, not long after my mother's death, she would visit me in the night and sing to me. I knew she was not carrying her pain anymore. Her essence was powerful and loving and I intuitively knew that we could now have a relationship free of the constraints of both our pasts. We were free to love unconditionally.

It is a powerful thing to experience. As I am now open to receiving her help and assistance, that enables me to receive her love, her gifts, and her skills, as well as the power of my ancestry. I ask for help regularly and she still gives me a telling off now and again. She keeps me in alignment when things sometimes take a dip, as in life as they naturally do.

After my mother passed, my relationship with my father changed and we got to know each other very well. We moved into total acceptance of each other. He supported me unconditionally and began to love me unconditionally. There was no judgement and no criticism, just acceptance.

It is so powerful, so beautiful to experience, and so freeing. My father passed away four years after my mother and these were the most healing years of my life. Through accepting myself and his acceptance of me, I healed enough to allow love in, in a bigger way.

How Understanding Heals

THE MAKING OF RELATIONSHIPS

IS AN UNBREAKABLE BOND

THAT WILL BE THE MAKING OF YOU.

My father had had several strokes after my mother's death but he was so strong. I felt he made a decision not to go with her but to stay here in physical form and assist us both to heal.

He fell ill on December 4th 2011, went into hospital on December 27th 2011, and never came back out again. He passed away on July 27th 2012. My partner came into my life on December 28th 2011.

As we grew closer together, my father's health deteriorated. He was letting go but it was not an easy process. He was so ill that I told him it was okay to go and that I wanted him to. I knew that he really did not want to stay here in physical form. I knew he and I struggled to let go of the control of each other because he loved his family so much. He loved me and I loved him.

What, at this point, neither of us had learned is that love is never lost, you do not need to control it, it is an ever flowing stream, it is eternal and so are all your relationships.

The relationship I have now with my parents is that I accept that they did the best they could. They enabled me to create a co- dependency that served me, as all our creation has a purpose. As I opened up to the truth of my higher purpose of my relationship with my parents, I dropped all the anger, resentment, and negative thoughts I had been holding on to. I chose to acknowledge and see their beauty and the amazing caring people they where, that's the truth. It did not benefit me to carry any emotion other than love. I dropped "You did this" and "You didn't do that" - stuff that had kept me in the place of victim.

The truth is, they played the perfect part for me. I chose them, I invited them to be my parents, I gave them the script. They served me well!

My relationship now with both my parents is powerful. They may not be here in physicality but their spirit is always around. My father assists my business and the work I do on Money Patterns. Finance was his talent and he was able to manifest money always.

My mother guides me into my Goddess power and so does my grandmother. I am blessed to have so much love in my life.

Healing With Your Ancestors

WHEN YOU MAKE PEACE WITH YOUR PAST YOU ARE REQUESTING NEW EXPERIENCES.

Your family did the best they could for you. When you understand them and their past experiences and heal your relationships, you will have a more loving relationship with the self.

Spiritually, you chose your parents so you could learn the perfect lessons that you agreed to learn. When you understand that what you have learnt is positive and beneficial to you, you will be free of past pain through your ability to view your parents and all your experiences in life differently.

Lineage healing allows you to move beyond forgiveness and into acceptance through your ability to understand yourself and your ancestors and the patterns that have been passed on through generations.

Sleeping with the myth of fear is over. You are awakening to the truth. It will set you free to soar to new heights.

It is paramount to your healing journey and to your creative spirit that you make peace with your parents, family, and ancestors - then make positive relations with them by connecting with their true spirit, devoid of the behaviours they have carried.

In life or death, healing can always be done. A person does not have to be here in physical form for you to heal your relationship with them. It is your heart you are opening.

You are healing with the energy of a higher emotional frequency that moves you from pain to gain. The frequency is pure love. You are healing with your higher self. You do not have to have the permission of the other person, nor do you have to do the healing with them. It only involves you.

It is a deep process, you are healing on a super conscious level that requires no physical communication or connection. It requires only an open heart from yourself, your ability to understand, and your commitment to heal yourself through the power of your inner wisdom and insight.

The Benefits Of Lineage Healing

Your family lineage is perfect for your learning, growth, and transformation. It is often the biggest teacher you will ever have.

Why Positive Relations Are Vital To Your Success

The making of relations is the foundation to your health, wealth, and abundance. That is simply because positive, loving relationships, based on compassion, insight, and understanding allow you to be happy, whole, and complete.

Happiness and freedom are the keys to opening the door to your unlimited potential. The making of relationships allow you to drop any emotion that will not serve you, and view the situation from a higher emotional and spiritual stance.

Unconditional love, unconditional acceptance in the making of positive relationships with all things, will lead you to a whole new way of life - a life that is prosperous. The making of relationships will make you a happier and healthier person... the two qualities that attract wealth.

For years I carried anger, blame and shame, self-denial and self-dislike. I blamed myself harshly for the mistakes I had made, although there are no mistakes in life, only lessons. I kept on carrying the shame, although there was no shame to carry. I carried on attracting controlling or co-dependent relations that stifled my freedom or brought me more pain.

Dealing With Anger

> IT'S OKAY TO FEEL AND EXPRESS,
>
> BUT THEN LET GO.

We are all doing the best we can in any given moment. We are all teachers, healers, and mentors for each other. Without each other there could be no growth. It is what makes you wake up to the truth of who you are - people are the miracles in your life. Your ancestry is your link to your transformation.

I felt very angry with my mother for not acknowledging what she wanted in life. As I desired to have more, she told me I was ungrateful and selfish. I felt caught up in inner turmoil and confusion about what was right and what was wrong.

My inner being wanted to escape this mess and yet I did not know how to - not knowing how to express who I was, not knowing how to give to myself, not knowing how to love and be loved. The not knowing was indeed a smoke screen for not allowing. Why? Because I feared my loving essence and the power within.

Through the beauty of my spiritual channel, I was enabled to understand the truth of my parents, why they were like they were. I took the responsibility for what I had created. I healed my relationship with my mother and my father. I now honour who they are, gentle spirits that want to help always. They love me and I adore them. They are now always with me in a powerful way, ready to help and assist. I am never alone.

Release Yourself From A Mindset That Keeps You In Pain

HOW YOU VIEW A PERSON OR SITUATION CAUSES THE PAIN, NOT THE EXPERIENCE. CHANGE YOUR UNDERSTANDING AND CHANGE THE PAIN TO GAIN.

To acknowledge the true essence of a person beyond their earthy physicality and beyond their experiences that formed their behaviour is the most rewarding experience you will ever have. It is unconditional love in its highest form. It will free you and open you up to feel much healthier emotions.

Why would you want to hold a belief (about someone who caused you pain) that probably is not the truth of the situation? Surrender your mindset and seek the deeper root of the issue. Open your heart to compassion and see only good.

Your Shoes, Their Shoes

NEVER JUDGE ANOTHER FOR
YOU KNOW NOT WHAT IT IS LIKE
IN THEIR SHOES.

When you gain the insight and inner wisdom into what it is like to walk in another's shoes you 'see them'. Spiritually, you will need to make a connection through the power of meditation, which connects your higher self and the higher self of the person you want to enter into the making of relations with.

Firstly, you will have to have a willingness to understand from another's shoes and make a commitment to implementing your new understanding into your new belief system.

You may choose not to enter into the making of relations with your lineage. Some of my clients find it too painful when they have experienced abuse. It is important to remember that this is about your healing.

First, it is about the love you hold for you. You are doing this for you, first and foremost. If you find that you have chosen not to enter into this process of making relations, be kind to yourself and give yourself permission to choose. For your own health and well-being, if you can accept the ***person*** and not what they did or how they behaved, then you are moving into freedom.

Wrap yourself up in a blanket of self-love. You are not here to tolerate anything or anyone that does not serve your highest good. You are here on this planet to live the life you love with the people you choose to enter into your sacred space.

Asking For The Assistance You Need

> HELP IS ALWAYS THERE FOR YOU.
> YOU ARE NEVER ALONE.
> YOUR ANCESTRY ARE POWERFUL.
> ASK THEM TO ASSIST YOU TO HEAL,
> EMPOWER, AND LEAD!

The making of relations gives you the privilege to gain insight into the pure loving power of your ancestry. As you now awake up to the truth of who they are, you 'see' your parents, grandparents, or great grandparents for what they are and not for what they were not.

So now you can ask for their help and support and receive the guidance that you need. Ask your ancestors and let them know what kind of support and help you require. Our loved ones are always with us and, on a spiritual level, only too happy to help! Ask silently like you would in prayer, then have the trust and faith to know that your request will be answered. All the love and support you need is always there for you.

Sacred Contracts

All that you have experienced has been perfect to bring you to this place of understanding. Now you can transform those experiences into the making of who you are.

Entering Into The Process Of The Making Of Relations

Take some time out for yourself in a quite space. Clear your mind of any thoughts and let your mind be open to new ways of viewing a situation. Do not have your mind **set**, be open and be flexible in your approach. Take onboard a new way of thinking and feeling as you create a new belief system that will support you and give you the truth of the situation.

It is so important at this stage to trust in your inner knowing and gut feeling, so you can begin to work with your higher consciousness.

You may feel you need some support from a friend as you enter into this process it can be a very emotional process and it is paramount that you give to yourself more love and more support. Or you may decide to work with a mentor or coach.

For more information on Lineage Healing workshops go to:

www.JulieAnneHart.com

The making of relations is your ability to heal your heart and free yourself from painful thoughts and toxic emotions that block you from love. You will set yourself free from the shackles of the past. As you do this, you free others and give them the choice to heal too.

When you heal with your ancestry with insight and understanding, you can then connect on a heart-to-heart level and see the truth in them and in yourself. In doing so, you make a connection with their true power and move on into empowerment.

Exercise

THE MAKING OF RELATIONS

You may need to have someone to support you through this process as it is an emotional one. It is important that you allow yourself to receive additional support and love, nurture yourself, and give yourself the time to reflect and simply ***be***.

Find a safe space where you will not be disturbed.

- ➢ Make your safe space neat and tidy to assist you to relax.
- ➢ Sit or lay somewhere comfortable and relax the mind. Let any thoughts draft away.
- ➢ Place your mind into neutral and think nothing at all.
- ➢ Take several deep breaths in and out to enable you to relax more.
- ➢ Focus on the family member you feel you need to enter into the making of relations with.
- ➢ Let your mind be creative. You must trust your intuition at this stage in the process.
- ➢ See yourself and this person standing together face-to-face.
- ➢ Now tell this person how you feel in a loving way. It is okay to express exactly how you feel.
- ➢ Now imagine that that person can speak back to you.

- ➢ Invite this person to tell you what life is like in their shoes and why they behaved as they did. Give them space and time to reply to you.
- ➢ Listen with understanding and compassion for both of you.
- ➢ Continue in conversation until you have both said what you needed to say.

What are your thoughts and feelings about this person now? How differently do you view your experiences now?

Are you ready to think and feel differently and enter into a loving belief system about the people in your life – a belief system that supports you?

I recommend that you keep a journal. You may need to repeat this exercise until you find the point of understanding and acceptance that brings you inner peace and harmony for yourself and others.

Lineage healing is about you healing your mind, body, and spirit. When you do this, you free yourself to love unconditionally and your relationships will change because you have changed.

You no longer harbour negative thoughts and feelings that keep you stuck with a closed heart. You are now free to move into self-empowerment and create and carve the life you love to lead.

You are here on this amazing planet to live happily, whole and complete. There are no restrictions to that, only what you chose to limit. Free yourself from your created limitations so you can take another step forwards and keep your wheel of life turning in the direction you choose to walk.

Affirmation

⌂ I am blessed. All is working out well. I see the truth in others, they see the truth in me.

Lineage healing can be a painful and traumatic process to go through alone. Give yourself the gift of support from a loved one. If you would like more information on how I can support you through a lineage healing workshops and Pure Love Pure Spirit retreats, go to:

www.JulieAnneHart.com

PART TWO

EMPOWERMENT

HOW TO SET YOURSELF FREE AND DANCE WITH LIFE

෨෬

Your creation is the spirit of you. Your spirit is your essence and identity. It is unique, it is awesome, it is beauty beyond belief. This is who you are. It's all in your hands.

You are the creator of your own destiny and you have unlimited possibilities and potential. You're your own magic genie, your wish is at your command, your empowerment is in your hands.

It's hard to believe this when your life doesn't feel or seem this way, when the road has been one that has been difficult to walk or when the road you are currently walking feels like climbing a never-ending hill.

You can do it! It will take determination and persistence but you already have these strengths - you must now choose to use them.

All the skills you need to empower yourself are inside you so lighten up, you can drop the heavy emotional load in any given moment. Know you are safe, protected, and looked after on a universal level.

We are now at a crossroads in our journey. As we move from the healing phase into the empowerment phase you will start to feel joy. You will feel uplifted and it will be as if a mist is clearing. The future is brighter with possibilities than you ever imagined.

This section of the book will empower you to take hold of those possibilities and show you how to shape them into what you desire.

Make Yourself A Priority

> MEET YOUR OWN NEEDS AND LIFE
> WILL MEET YOU THERE TOO - THAT'S
> THE MAGIC OF THE UNIVERSE.

For me, my empowerment journey meant me taking the action and going and getting what I wanted in life with the determination not to stop until I achieved it.

The ingrained familiarity of my family programme and pattern - ask for nothing and accept your lot in life - had taken away the gift of me giving to myself. As I awakened more to my spiritual power, the feelings of passion, inspiration, and a deep desire to be my potential filled my inner being like nothing before.

I had done many years of personal and professional development but personal empowerment is different - it connects you with the spirit of the self.

Make Friends With Your Fear

NOTHING CAN BE ELIMINATED BUT EVERYTHING CAN BE TRANSFORMED INTO AN ASSET.

I needed to allow in more love, more success, and more abundance and face my fear. Moving into a bigger business and being seen was a big thing for me but I did not always acknowledge my fear.

Fear is often hidden or unseen. I projected my fear onto external issues or I blamed it on someone else.

Opening my heart to a loving relationship pushed all my buttons totally, I felt every ounce of my fear. My fear manifested itself in so many different ways. Fear is so intelligent and clever at trying to keep you safe, safe in the same comfort of what you have always experienced but this was not comfortable for me any longer, I craved more.

In order to receive more I had to wake up to what was happening. I had to wake up to my program of fear and change by pattern of behaviour. You cannot eliminate your fear, you have to make it your friend, ask your fear to support you in a different way and carry on building the life you love.

I had stayed asleep where receiving money was concerned. I was unconsciously aware of my program. My primary money emotions were guilt and shame. Those emotions had blocked the flow of my prosperity and limited my potential.

Be Kind To Yourself

> KINDNESS IS LIKE LIGHTING A CANDLE.
> YOU SHINE WHEREVER YOU GO.

I took my self empowerment a step at a time and just gave myself the permission to receive and do the things I needed to do. I worked on surrendering and releasing all the emotions, thoughts, and feelings associated with fear. I said yes to life itself, I carried on walking in the direction I wanted to go regardless of my current situation.

I never allowed anyone or anything to stand in my way. I never allowed the lack of money to stop me or others opinions to block or limit me. I became strong. I released and surrendered my fear to the universe and stretched myself into becoming the new me.

Love Yourself A Little More Each Day

> LOVE IS MAGNETIC.
> IT HAS A PULL, A FORCE.
> LET LOVE IN AND BE A MAGNET OF ATTRACTION.

Self-empowerment is self-love. It will take strength, courage, and your commitment to make your outcome implicit, regardless of what challenges you face. Remember, there are no blocks or barriers, only those created in your myth of fear. It's just you stood in your own way.

You can choose to see your challenges as one of two things:

> - You can view it as your fear (YOU) getting in the way, or ...
> - You can view it as a gift to you that you can reflect and learn from that will aid your growth to heal and become more empowered.

Chose to believe that things are working out for you and they will. Believe otherwise and they will not.

The law is simple!

Communicate With The Self In A Loving, Positive Way

SELF TALK IS POWERFUL SO DROP THE CRITICAL PARENT IN YOU AND LET THE YOUR WISE SPIRIT SPEAK

I found my mind again and again would tell me a million reasons why I could not or should not do something. I had to speak back to my myth of fear. I decided to give my myth of fear a name and, lovingly, I would reassure us both. It was the part of me that feared my power on all levels. I reassured her so she and I could grow.

Be aware of what messages you gift to yourself and speak lovingly as you gently empower yourself into creating and experiencing your heart's desire.

Get Clear On Your Heart's Desire

Clarity is insight, intuition, wisdom and, most of all, it is your heart-centred passion. It's your fire energy, the spark of creation that dwells within you, bursting with life-force to come out.

Clarity and a strong intention are key factors in your 'self'-empowerment to create your heart's desire and live the life you love. Clarity must come first. Without it you are in the fog of confusion and you now know what that is… FEAR. You know why you created it!

So stop, take some time out and introspect the self to get the clarity you need to empower your own self-created reality.

Deep inside of me there was a calling, a strong desire to change and I could not ignore it. It was so strong. The time had come when I loved myself enough to say yes to myself, yes to life, yes to unleashing all my potential, and yes to the unlimited opportunities I desired to experience:

- ➢ I desired to have a successful business.
- ➢ I desired to live in the country in a beautiful setting and place.
- ➢ I desired to have healthy relationships with all things.
- ➢ I desired to love and be loved.
- ➢ I desired to have a life partner.
- ➢ I desired to give to myself.

This was a new way of honouring me, of giving to me, of allowing myself to receive. It was the breakthrough point of saying I AM WORTHY.

Stepping Out Of The Old And Into The New

DEATH AND REBIRTH IS A NATURAL CYCLE UPON MOTHER EARTH.
YOU ARE PART OF THIS CYCLE.
TO HOLD ONTO THE OLD IS TO NEVER SEE THE BEAUTY OF THE NEW.

Change, change, all change everything must go! Your empowerment journey is different to your healing journey. It is you accepting only what you want in your life. It is you knowing exactly what you desire to create. It is you moving out of the old experiences and into the new experiences.

Empowerment is your journey to self-belief.

Through empowerment you heal on a deeper level. Empowerment will push all your buttons and, for some people, empowerment is too much for them to handle. They do not progress past their healing journey and their creation is stagnant.

Some of the most powerful, spiritually-gifted people I have worked with have thrown in the towel at this stage or have chosen not to progress beyond the healing journey which allows them to stay in the old story.

Heal, then move into empowerment, then you will keep leaping more into your leadership. You are so powerful!

You will need to integrate a new way of being into your **conscious awareness**.

It is vital, if you want to leap into leadership, that you now stretch into more of your truth and make changes in all areas of your life. Wake up, be aware. The old myth of fear will be around the corner so watch your actions and behaviour, thoughts, and feelings.

Responsibility

> RESPONSIBILITY IS CHOICE,
> IT IS FREEDOM.
> THE ROAD OF RESPONSIBILITY
> IS EMPOWERMENT.

Responsibility is your ability to respond - **not react** - to any challenge, situation, person, or place.

Responsibility is you taking ownership of yourself, your life, and your creation.

Responsibility is you taking charge of your actions and commitments.

Responsibility is you using your insight and understanding to benefit you.

Responsibility is to know your truth and implement it.

Responsibility leaves no room for blaming others or shaming the self.

Responsibility is your ability to view every situation from a stance that you are the creator of what you experience. That will allow you to take responsibility to empower the self.

Responsibility means you are now creating the experiences that you do want and when you experience what you don't want it is your responsibility to end the cycle.

All your experiences are a mirror to understanding the self. Responsibility means nothing is an external factor, everything comes from within you. Moving into self-empowerment is a progressive, step-by-step process with self love, nurture, and care for oneself. Each step of the way will bring you more understanding of who you are and the work that you will need to do.

ALL IS WELL. YOUR DREAMS ARE COMING - BIGGER THEN YOU THINK.

Responsibility is yours to own. It is your commitment to your journey to more love, success, and abundance.

When you ask 'how and why' you are getting in your own way. Move out of your own way by taking the responsibility to have a belief system that supports your goals. Have more trust and faith in your ability to create and achieve your desired outcomes. Have:

- ➢ The discernment to know what action you need to take.
- ➢ The commitment to an inspired action plan.
- ➢ The commitment to implement your actions into the outcomes your heart desires.
- ➢ The courage to keep going when the going gets tough.

It is your responsibility to:
- ➢ Be out there and active.
- ➢ Be happy, whole, and complete.
- ➢ Be seen (stop hiding).
- ➢ Get your message out.
- ➢ Follow your heart-centred passion.
- ➢ Be Focused.
- ➢ Be Organised.
- ➢ Love yourself enough to receive.
- ➢ Love your creation.

Responsibility is self love that acts as your guardian.

Dancing with life is just like being invited to a grand ball. But you have to get dressed and be ready to go; not sat at home in the kitchen just wishing.

It is in the knowing and the doing that the transformation occurs.

Say Yes To Yourself

GIVE YOURSELF PERMISSION TO LIVE.
ARE YOU DANCING WITH LIFE
OR ARE YOU DITHERING?

Saying "I cannot do this because …" is saying "I do not want to do it!"

"I can't," also means "I don't want to."

Once you are clear on what you desire to achieve in your life or business or relationships, then you have to say YES to it! Yes leads you into self-empowerment. YES is giving yourself permission to say yes to yourself and the life you want to lead. There is magic in the yes word because it means you are beginning to believe.

When you say yes to yourself the universe opens the doors to delivering you the opportunity you desire. You say yes and the universe says yes back.

I have never ever said no to myself.

I allowed myself to take the journey knowing that I was safe. Saying yes to you increases your trust and faith in yourself. How can you become an empowered leader of your own life if you cannot say yes to your journey to your unlimited potential?

It will be fearful to say yes to yourself so take several deep breaths in and out until the fear eases. As you now give yourself permission, as you release the fear, you will stretch and feel more of the truth of who you are. So learn to love that feeling.

Saying yes to yourself is the beginning of bridging the gap from where you are to where you want to go. My journey of filling in the gap has been a rollercoaster ride but I stayed on it. I only wish I had lightened up and laughed more.

Worry is lack of faith. Worry is not real, it is fear and it does not exist - only in the myth of your mind. Bridging the gap from where you are to where you want to go means leading your life in its fullest form.

This requires you to implement two things:

- ➢ Your ability to love yourself enough to say yes and then keep taking the action.
- ➢ Your ability to receive more love, more success, and more abundance.

I was not good at receiving.

It was something I had been so unfamiliar with and it has been a progression into opening my heart to love and receive love. A journey of deserving more.

There have been times when I was not awake to even knowing that I desired or deserved more than I was experiencing. As I experienced more of what I did not want, it was a gift because it allowed me to take an introspection of myself.

As I began to connect with my feelings, I began to listen to myself. I allowed my emotions to be my guide and, when I did not feel good about certain things, it was always the indicator that something was out of alignment with my worth. The key for me was not to ignore my feelings but to understand them and act upon them.

What To Do When The Going Gets Tough

FAITH AND TRUST MOVE MOUNTAINS.

LET YOURSELF HAVE IT

AND THEN EXPERIENCE IT.

There have been times when I just wanted to run away. It has been exhausting, exciting, explosive, and downright hard work at times. The healing breaks down the old myth of fear. Your empowerment is a breakthrough, it's your birthing process. Like any birthing, it is always a miracle in form.

Frustration, confusion, and conflict are all part of your journey. You will have the frustration of not receiving and changing quick enough. The confusion of how to get where you desire to go and the conflict with the parts of the self that want to change and the parts of the self that want to protect you and not change.

It's a whirl of emotions. When this happens, spend some time in nature, take some time to go within to seek your inner wisdom. Ask yourself some questions and seek the answers to them as you connect with your higher self.

Acknowledge your fear, then stay focused on where you are heading so you can stay on your sacred path of creating what you love.

No Excuses

EXCUSES FEED YOUR FEAR.

YOUR FEAR LOVES EXCUSES

AND YOUR FEAR IS HUNGRY FOR THEM.

Freedom from fear is your ability to know what you are feeding your soul with. Feed your soul divine love - only loving messages and daily reassurance.

You cannot eliminate fear or push it away, you have to acknowledge it. Get to know it, have a relationship with it, and then you can coach it and mentor it until it is on your side.

As you make a relationship with fear and you understand it is your fear, you will come to know the voice of fear speaking through you. You will begin to know that fear isn't true, it's a myth.

It is paramount that you listen to your intuition.

There is a fine line between intuition and fear. You can separate the fear voice and the voice of your intuition. At first they are often misinterpreted. You will mistake fear for your gut feeling telling you something but it's not, it's fear calling.

To access your intuition, you will have to practice listening to your heart and not to your head.

As you learn to do this you will then be able to feel the difference between the message or fear and your intuition. Your intuition will always give you a clear, strong message. So will your fear. Your intuition is the strongest if you give it time to speak through you.

No excuse means just that: **no** excuses. So "I can't because ..." or "If only I could" are excuses. They are your fear speaking for you. Acknowledge it, recognise it, then do the thing you were making excuses for anyway.

Let yourself make empowered decisions. Indecisiveness is fear. Use the power of self-talk and affirmations to assist you to re-program.

It is so important to know that you are being guided and blessed as you walk this journey. There is a higher power, a spiritual energy force that supports you, so hand over the control. Surrender and release to source energy. It knows the bigger picture.

Never put off taking action. Do it when you are inspired and not the day after or you are just resisting your creative power. Resistance, impatience, and sabotage are all fear-based behaviours.

When you make an excuse you are saying "No" to yourself! You are connected to your myth of fear.

How The Intelligent Universe Works

> BECOME THE MYSTERY. SEE IT. FEEL IT, BELIEVE IT, AND YOU SHALL RECEIVE IT.

There is a higher power so intelligent, so all-knowing, all-seeing, all-understanding, all-singing, and dancing. It knows so much more than you do. It holds the bigger picture.

You must have a vision so know what you want. Get into the feel of it, live it and let your emotional health increase. Then surrender the picture to the higher power.

There is no need to control your outcome, just know it is on its way. The universe knows exactly what your needs are and how to get you from A to Z.

Surrender and release. Hand over your doubt, your worries, your fears and know that the universe is looking after you on your journey to your unlimited potential. The universe will deliver to you exactly what you need to take you where you desire to go. So let it, it's far more intelligent than us humans.

Drop the control, let go of the picture and move into the mystery of life.

Understanding Energy

Everything on the planet is energy. There is only one stream of creative life-force energy, that stream is love.

When you are in fear, you make a connection with negative, fear-based energy. As you begin to wake up, you are making a connection with the stream of positive loving energy that is all encompassing, creative energy. This will yield to you and your desires in physical form. As you move into empowerment, you will move backwards and forwards between the two streams. It is impossible to be connected to both streams at any one given point.

To move into the stream of positive loving energy, you will have to make changes in your life now. Firstly you will have to have the ability to think lovingly, see with loving insight, and feel with no fear.

To do this it often requires total change of everything you are currently experiencing. Your environment may need to change, the area you live in or the work that you do may need to change. The people you associate with, your relationships, everything in your life will have to support you. To be connected to the stream of positive loving energy, every experience has to be a happy one, or viewed from a positive perspective.

Otherwise, you will automatically move back into the negative stream of fear-based energy.

Staying connected to the stream of positive loving energy will lift your spirit so high you will soar. Watch out for the magic of the universe at work and take note now on how much more inspired you are beginning to feel. Be really vigilant to look out for opportunities that will come your way.

Get Invested

HONOUR AND RESPECT YOURSELF! GIVE UNTO YOU AND PUT YOURSELF FIRST.

I knew I needed a mentor and, as soon as I made a decision to invest in one, she came into my life.

On many occasions this has happened to me: I decide to do something and the universe makes it available to me.

My intuition told me to be discerning and seek advice from people who supported my journey only, as I had had a tendency to seek out people who reinforced my myth of fear.

With both the healing and the empowerment work, you will need some support, someone you can talk to, someone who understands you. This may be a friend, family member, or colleague. You will need to choose a person with a positive outlook who is committed to their journey of living life in their potential. Find someone who is prepared to feel their own fear and change anyway.

You may decide to invest in a mentor or coach.

I have on several occasions. I needed to - it is deep work you are doing and it will require a professional or a person who has walked this journey to aid you. Investing in yourself is you loving you on a deeper level. It is you saying "Yes" and taking responsibility to move energetically into the new.

Your life experiences will begin to change. At first maybe they will change slowly but they will change. You will need to honour the new changes, however small they may be it is change. Hold the feeling of gratitude and appreciation for what has shown up in your life. Your perception and mindset has to be in alignment now with the new you, not the old you.

The new ways of being must be implemented daily for the transformation to birth itself fully. It's wild and it's radical but lighten the load and allow yourself to have fun. Life's a game, make it a pleasurable one, it's your playground.

You are now ready to walk a path of beauty. You will have to shed the old you, the way you once thought and felt.

FEAR IS DEBILITATING,

LOVE IS EMPOWERING.

You are now at a crossroads. You are about to take the transformation into walking your own path of beauty. It's simple when you know how.

Exercise

SELF EMPOWERMENT

This exercise may seem very simple but it is very powerful. By turning your focus away from what has been keeping you in fear, and seeing that the reality is very different, that you are someone who has achieved, who has talent and potential, then you will be able to live in that potential as we continue the journey.

- Make sacred space for yourself. A place where you will not be disturbed. Make it comfortable, tidy, and clean so it feels good for you to relax in.
- Sit or lie comfortably and relax.
- Place your mind into neutral and think nothing.
- Now bring your attention to yourself. Think about all your achievements, talents, and skills.
- Congratulate yourself on your strength and courage and the determination that has brought you to this point on your journey.
- Take several deep breaths in and out.
- Breathe into your solar plexus and breathe out. It holds your gut feelings, your inner knowing and intuition.
- Ask this powerful intuitive part of you for the guidance you need right now.
- Trust your intuition and your feelings - it is your wisdom giving you the answers.

Keep a journal of your experiences and repeat the exercise as many times as you need to.

Affirmation

- I walk a path of beauty.
- I choose to see only beauty behind me and in front of me.
- I am free.

TAKING THE LEAP INTO YOUR UNLIMITED POTENTIAL

How to walk a path of beauty and stay on it

୨୦୧୫

Listen To Your Soul Calling

AS YOU LISTEN TO YOUR HEART'S DESIRE, TAKE NOTICE. IT IS CALLING YOU TO STEP UP INTO THE TRUE SPIRIT OF YOU AND BECOME YOUR FULL POTENTIAL.

My heart yearns to create and make a difference. I hold a burning desire to do it and achieve it. It is an energy with intense feeling that is impossible to ignore. It is my soul calling me to be my truth with the acceptance of nothing less.

Part of me still wants the little girl in me to stay the same: safe, secure, and familiar with her surroundings, dependent on others' thoughts, opinions and guidance, wanting acceptance through pleasing.

The power part of me wants to fling out my arms and sweep the old stuff well out of the way.

The higher self, the spiritual part of me desires to see - and only see - the total truth of who I am.

This is the journey you will take but, believe me, it is the most amazing journey you will never walk. It is the journey to the self, to your magnificence in all its forms.

It is the spiritual part of me that carries me forward with trust and faith. I ask for assistance from the universe to assist me on my climb. That allows me to let go and implicitly know that what I ask for is being delivered.

There have been so many days and nights where my thinking has been out of alignment with my inner truth. I have worried, doubted, and panicked over bills, business, and money. I have felt like a fraud, a failure, and a fake - none of which are true.

I am so powerful, so connected to source energy and yet, when I needed it the most, I have not connected to this powerful source energy that is love. I have not allowed myself to be reassured. In essence it is quite abusive because what I was doing again was withholding love.

When I awoke to this pattern I stopped it. I surrendered and released the doubt to a higher power and allowed a loving, spiritual power to be my guide.

There is one final step that will take that feeling of empowerment and will allow you to use it to create your own vision. To bring what you want into your life. To live in your joy. It isn't enough just to feel empowered. We want to create a new reality. To see what is possible when we are fully awake to the potential. This section shows you how to do that.

Freedom To Fly

> YOUR POTENTIAL IS UNDERSTOOD THROUGH ACKNOWLEDGING YOUR PASSION. THEN YOU CAN FULFIL YOUR HIGHER PURPOSE.

I desire to share my knowledge, life experiences, and inner wisdom for the highest good to assist others. Mother Earth calls me to hear her messages and I am not afraid to listen, to acknowledge, and - most important - to share it with others to make a bigger difference.

Dropping the myth of fear is freedom of expression. You take the mask off completely and be your authentic self. It is the only way to reach your potential. Being awake to who you are and really seeing you with understanding and insight will allow your potential to soar. If you are going to create a path of beauty and be your potential there is no room for negative emotions and self-criticism.

Aim High

> TO SEE THE TRUTH OF WHO YOU ARE
> AND THE GIFTS YOU HAVE IS BLISSFUL.

To use your gifts with meaning and purpose is to feel a completion of oneself within - where you always feel at one with the universe.

The more you acknowledge yourself, the more you will desire to achieve and reach your potential. You will want to seek out your purpose so you can feel whole and complete. You will want to seek out your purpose so you can assist others. You will want to use all your skills and abilities. You will feel this desire very strongly so do not resist it!

Whatever you are passionate about doing in life, create it, start the journey towards it. Whether you choose to learn a new skill, change career, start a new business, or have the relationship of your dreams, listen to what you want to do and do it!

Holding back is procrastination and it is your fear standing in your way, so pay no attention to it and proceed forward. Stop thinking you will fail, that's your fear. There is no failure, there is no fear. When you walk this path and stay on it, you are walking a road that will lead you to your heart's desire.

Failure only comes when you choose to stop walking.

Walking The Path Of Beauty

TO WALK A PATH OF BEAUTY IS TO LEAVE A TRAIL OF BEAUTY BEHIND YOU IN FRONT OF YOU THAT WILL ASSIST GENERATIONS TO COME.
YOUR BLUEPRINT UPON THE PLANET IS NEEDED.

I am now free to keep on moving, enjoying my creation, and seeing it form. Your unlimited potential, like mine, is your ability to 'see', to have the insight to know the planet is powerful and so are you!

You have to love yourself a little more each day so your self-esteem and inner confidence is heightened enough to say "Yes" to yourself, "Yes" I deserve more, and "Yes" I expect more, and "Yes" I am worthy, and I am going hell out to get it.

Love big. You will have to be awake to your feelings, they will reflect your beliefs. If you feel good and have no problem in taking the action to what you want to create, you have no resistance. You will resist what you fear. Be aware, stay awake to your thoughts, feelings, and behaviour. If they are not supporting you then affirm a thought that gives you a new belief.

Focus Only On Where You Are Heading

THINK NOT OF WHERE YOU ARE RIGHT NOW. YOUR NEEDS WILL BE MET.

You are being looked after, so vision the future your heart desires, then feel the feeling of it in the power of the present.

As you move into being and living your unlimited potential, you will gain inner strength and come to know your own mind, body, and spirit in a deeper and more purposeful way. Believe in yourself, listen to your intuition. It will bring to you the passion and inspiration to keep you walking in the direction you desire to go with organisation and focus.

It is my spiritual connection and direct channel that provides me with the guidance, the trust, and faith to keep walking my path of beauty and following my heart's desire to live the life I love. As I make a regular deep connection to a Mother Earth spirituality, she gives to me her strength. She feeds me, she holds me.

Through my spiritual connection I have grown, healed, and taken the transformation. It is through this connection, coupled with self love, determination, and an inner knowing that all is well that keeps me in the stream of loving, positive energy that brings my unlimited potential to my door. I receive it with gratitude.

Your unlimited potential lies in your ability to 'see' the truth of who you are. To walk a path of beauty is to 'see' the beauty in what is all around you and to know what is coming to you! Then you have surrendered your myth of fear and opened your heart to love.

Move Beyond The Power Of Belief

> TO WALK A BEAUTY PATH IS TO MOVE BEYOND BELIEF INTO THE KNOWING OF ALL THAT IS – THEN YOU WILL HAVE BLISSFUL FREEDOM TO BE TO DO AND TO HAVE.

Beyond the power of belief lies implicit knowing. It is a strong energy force within you called determination where you do not tolerate an outcome anything less than what you desire.

The most powerful moments in my life have been when I have implicitly known that I will do something and it will happen. I have made the outcome non-negotiable. When you do this, you move to a higher emotional level because you feel good. You feel strong, you feel in your power. You are in total truth and faith you will flow with the stream of positive loving energy. You will be a magnet of attraction.

Purifying your belief system and your spiritual belief system acts as a filter in which fear cannot seep through. Make your outcomes non-negotiable. Do not settle for second best. Expect the best, be your best, and know that the best has yet to be delivered.

Spirit I Am

> AS YOU COME TO KNOW YOUR OWN SPIRIT YOU DISCOVER A WHOLE NEW YOU.

We are all spiritual beings having a human experience. To walk a path of beauty will require you to take daily meditations to assist you to remove the confusion and gain the clarity, insight, and inner wisdom that come from entering the silence and listening to the higher self.

The more you meditate, the more you still and quieten the mind, the more you can move your focus on to what you desire and not what you are experiencing in the moment. Your focus will bring you inspiration to assist your organisational skills to take the action you need to.

Dealing With The Demon Of Doubt

> THE UNIVERSE IS SUPPORTING YOUR CLIMB. WHY WASTE YOUR ENERGY ON THE DEMON OF DOUBT THAT DOES NOT EXIST? IT ONLY EXISTS IN THE MIND MYTH OF YOUR FEAR.

The one big enemy to your unlimited potential is **doubt**.

It will wipe out your new belief system and stop you from walking your path of beauty. Doubt has no place in your life. Doubt is indecisiveness. It is lack of trust and faith in yourself and in the universe.

When doubt surfaces, you are questioning yourself so now is the time to show yourself exactly what you believe in and give doubt one big message - your inner truth. Tell doubt your new beliefs and allow yourself to be comforted by your new beliefs and the doubt will ease.

Seek guidance from those that support you and love you. Listen to yourself. You are powerful, you know exactly what is right for you so listen to that voice minus the doubt. Increase your faith in yourself, have faith in the universe, trust in yourself and your ability to make empowered choices.

Stand strong in your own shoes and remember you are never alone when the going gets tough. Sometimes it will help to ask for help and support from the power of your ancestry. Send out a prayer. Use your own empowerment tools of affirmation and meditation. Tell yourself the truth to support the new you and your new emerging lifestyle.

Connecting To A Mother Earth Spirituality

> MOTHER, I FEEL YOU UNDER MY FEET
> MOTHER, I HEAR YOUR HEART BEAT.
> YOU ARE NURTURED AND CARED FOR.

The richness of life comes though seeing the beauty of creation. You are part of that creation, you are a creator! Go into nature and just take a look. You have abundance everywhere. Mother Earth feeds all her children, she is abundant.

All your needs are provided for on this planet. Look at how magical the seasons are, how powerful the elements are, how beautiful the animals, trees and plants are – drink it in and let Mother Earth Feed you. She sees your beauty so honour her and see her as she sees you. Then you are rich, then you will have opened the door to the art of true prosperity.

Making a physical and spiritual connection to nature will increase your intuition and inner knowing. As you take time out to be at one with Planet Earth, you will come to know Mother Earth in a deeper way and she will assist you to find a deeper level of clarity, wellness, and prosperity.

As you connect with Mother Earth, it will also deepen your connection with the spirit of the self.

Staying On The Path Of Beauty

HAPPINESS OPENS UP YOUR UNLIMITED POTENTIAL AND KEEPS YOU IN ALIGNMENT WITH YOUR INNER TRUTH.

Happiness is the way to walk the beauty path. With happiness and a free spirit you cannot walk another way, for these qualities keep you on it.

Sing your favourite song, do your favourite things, and keep on walking. Leading starts with allowing yourself to get happy. It means you have to keep walking.

"Rome wasn't built in a day," my father would tell me. I am a fire sign and the Aries in me gets impatient. If you really do believe, if you really want this path, if you are making it implicit then there is no stepping off.

As with any walk you would take, you wouldn't want to take a walk in nature in a beautiful part of the country moaning and groaning, complaining, and being unhappy. Would anyone want to walk with you? Probably not. The Universe feels the same.

When you are speaking what is not then you receive what is not. You are cutting off your connection to Mother Earth feeding you happiness. With happiness comes health, wealth, and prosperity. Walking the path to your unlimited potential is the same. Walk it happily.

Keep on walking. Keep on waking up to all that life has to offer you. The more you empower the self, the more happier, whole and complete you become. The more inspired action you take to transform the self, the more results you will see. Acknowledge them all. The small changes often turn out to be the most profound ones.

Take a moment to reflect on the enlightenment and understanding you now have about YOU! Are you ready to open up to being and receiving more? It's time to open your heart to your purpose, potential, and spiritual power. Life will never be the same again!

Exercise

The power of creative visioning

Allow yourself 30 minutes in a quite space where you will not be disturbed

- ➢ Sit comfortably and relax.
- ➢ Clear your mind of thoughts.
- ➢ Focus your attention onto yourself, your life, and business.
- ➢ Expand your creative mindset by allowing yourself to 'vision', to see images. Hold the picture in your mind of what your life will look like. Imagine the perfect business or career.
- ➢ Fill in all the details with the power of your imagination and feel it. Acknowledge how good it feels.
- ➢ Now say "Yes" to receive the life of your dreams, knowing you deserve it.
- ➢ Take several deep breaths in and out and just let yourself be reassured.
- ➢ Be happy.

Affirmation

✎ I allow myself to follow my path of unlimited potential. As I do this I create my own path of beauty.

PART THREE

LEADERSHIP

BIG HEART, BIG PURPOSE, BIG POWER

Your essence is love, your spirit is love, and self love is all that you need to allow yourself to live the dream.

❧

Open up your big heart and you open up to your even bigger purpose, it's the power of you, it's your capacity to love and to create.

Love has no boundaries. But what exactly is love? The planet we live on and share is love, every opportunity is love, happiness is love, your potential is love, your life is love, you are love, you are divine love.

We as human beings have the ability to channel divine love and to receive divine love to create peace, joy, harmony, healing, and abundance for everyone. Love is the creator, God, Buddha, whatever name you choose it to be. You are a part of that creation. You are a powerful creative spiritual being with a gift that is here to be used for a purpose. Just stop and think about what you are going to go on to achieve.

At this stage of our journey you should be feeling very different to the person you started as. If you want to take the time to go back through the stages of healing and empowerment, then do that. Take all the time you need for this journey.

In this stage of the book I am going to show you how to step into your true potential, how to live as the person you have become, and how to open your heart to the wonder of life.

Love, Live, And Be Happy

Happiness is your birthright so embrace it!

For me, I know my path is now open to love and receive beyond my wildest dreams. My mind sometimes does question this reality, a difficult belief to hold all the time.

Each day is Christmas day, the feeling of love and joy and excitement fills my being totally. I live in a beautiful place in the country with the person I love and in a way that I love. My lifestyle is blissful, I love my business and the people I see.

I now have to sit and think, "Wow! Is this really all for me?" Yes, it is all for me. Why? Because the universe loves me and it loves you too and it will deliver you your wildest dreams if you stay on your journey and walk the path of beauty.

I am blessed with the wisdom of my journey so I can share it with others so we all can move into the stream of positive loving energy. Take a moment and reflect on your inner passion to make a difference with the gifts and talents you have. Our planet is in need of more love and the more you create it through using your gifts and talents, the more you serve in a spiritual way.

Open Your Heart To Life

> CHOOSE ONLY WHAT YOUR HEART DESIRES TO EXPERIENCE.

Make a difference now and experience how beautiful can life be. I remember my father telling me that if you do not get things right in life, life can be cruel. I felt the fear of this statement, not daring to make a decision, not daring to choose, in my connection with my father. I know what he meant was that if you love yourself you are in total awe of life and you don't create pain.

I wake up each morning and thank God for this wonderful planet I live on. I see the trees, the green grass, the simple things that make the richness of life and form true prosperity.

> IT IS NOT WHAT YOU DO NOT HAVE THAT IS THE PROBLEM – IT IS YOUR INABILITY TO SEE WHAT IS ALREADY THERE.

Who knows where life will now take me? I am open to experiencing more wonderful things in a way that brings the wonder of a child to my every moment and finally I acknowledge I am love and I am lovable.

What a ride! One I would not change as it has made the uniqueness of me. I look back and I am thankful of all my experiences. They have given me so much and made me the person I am. My past is my success and my future is my love and the utilisation of this loving energy will become the foundation for others to heal. The grand design, your bigger picture, your prayers have been answered and dreams do come true.

Big Heart

EXPAND YOUR LOVE OUT.

An open heart that holds no grudge or past burden is open to receive more love, more success, and more abundance. If you are still holding on to anger, resentment, jealousy, and negative self emotions you will cut off your supply of divine love.

An open heart is passionate about life and will be lovingly determined to let it in. An open heart doesn't hold back! Expanding your heart is your capacity to love yourself and love the opportunities that come to you. Say "Yes!" to them with appreciation.

An open heart feels love. If you have followed the journey in this book you will have opened your heart and released the past. Keep acknowledging how far you have travelled. Keep on seeing and feeling only good. If you focus on what is not, you are closing down to love. Love is the creative energy force that will yield your desires into your reality.

Big Purpose

YOU ARE HERE WITH A MISSION.

Your mission is to discover the truth of who you are, what you are here to do, and then allow yourself to become it. Your purpose is so much bigger then you are currently aware of.

There is so much more to you then you realise. You are here to make a difference, you are a leader and a catalyst. You have spent years in the myth of fear creating experiences to hide your truth under. Now is the time to shine. All your life experiences are usable and form your bigger purpose. You have to be prepared to play a bigger game and stand on your soap box. It is not your ego, it is your truth. You know it, so own it.

Your purpose and prosperity are interlinked, you cannot have one without the other. Most creative and spiritual people fear their gifts and talents and hide them or minimise them. Most creative and spiritual people can be alien to money and view it as not spiritual.

Money is just a creative flow of loving energy that you receive for giving value to another. Really acknowledge what you have to offer, acknowledge all your learning and inner wisdom, and then make a decision on what you want to achieve. Think big - you cannot assist, support, or empower another if you are not in your true purpose or potential.

I find it so interesting that you want your loved ones to be their potential and live their purpose - it starts with you doing it first! You will have to walk your talk and talk your walk, but it is an amazing journey to share.

Big Power

You have the power to create unlimited opportunities.

You are part of this creative universe. You are powerful, it's time to stand in your powerfulness and embrace it.

You are a magnificent creator. You are a part of the creation of the universe. When you develop your connection to source, the spiritual power that is within you is activated and your intuition and inner knowing is triggered. You hold the capacity and capability to create unlimited opportunities - this is how powerful you are.

Meditate daily and begin the process of developing your spiritual connection. Ask for guidance, listen with love to the messages you receive. You will receive the answer you seek and it will come to you in many ways.

Listen to the message your solar plexus, your stomach, your gut feeling is telling you.

Learn to vision what you desire to create. If you cannot see your creation you cannot receive it. You ability to vision is your clarity. Gratefully receive what is given and you will then be open to receive more.

Creativity or Destruction?

BE AWARE OF YOUR DEMONS OF DESTRUCTION.

The creative spirit is a loving, powerful force. You are this force. Your ability to create is as easy as your ability to destroy. Creative people can destroy their create power and purpose very easily.

You are now taking the lead in your own creation so keep awake and be aware that any conflict, crisis, or difficulty will be the destructive side of fear showing up.

Conflict is also an indicator that you are out of alignment with the truth of who you are. It's okay, you just need to not buy into it. Acknowledge it but do not feed it.

This is a powerful time on our planet, it really is the land of opportunity and plenty. To rubbish, bin, or disregard your gifts and talents will never lead you into loving, abundant leadership.

To moan and groan about what is not showing up in your life is to not validate the gifts of Mother Earth assisting you.

YOU CANNOT LEAD FROM A PLACE OF VICTIM.

To criticise, shame, or blame the self or another will not open your heart to lead in life and business.

The Beauty Of You

> LET YOUR POTENTIAL OUT.
> BE YOUR HIGHER PURPOSE.
> STAND IN YOUR SPIRITUAL POWER.
> SIMPLY BE.

I once thought I was nothing, now I know I am everything and it feels amazing. You can do it too, you have already discovered so much about yourself.

Everything in life is dual night and day, pain and pleasure, happiness and sadness. With each duality you have the power to choose which side you face. If you are ready to experience abundance you must come to understand it and then choose it to know it.

There is so much love for each of us and it's so overwhelmingly powerful to receive it. You have been alien to love. Your fear once protected you from it. You had an innate ability to feel fear - now you have an innate ability to give and receive love.

It is your birthright.

Exercise

RITE OF PASSAGE CEREMONY

Find a quite place outdoors, maybe your garden or a field, a place where you will not be disturbed.

- ➢ Take a moment to think about the warmth of the sun and its purpose on the planet.

Big Heart, Big Purpose, Big Power

- The sun is fire energy, bringing warmth, passion, insight, enlightenment, and growth
- Take a moment to think about the water and its purpose on the planet.
- The water is cleansing, flowing, moving energy. Your body needs its life-force.
- Take a moment to think about Mother Earth and all that she provides.
- Take a moment to think about the sky each passing day, each cloud, the wind, a gentle breeze that blows the old away.
- Now honour this creation and know that you are part of it.
- Now ask that the fire brings you more heart-centred passion, inspiration, and clarity.
- The water brings you cleansing and movement into the new.
- The earth brings you more health, well-being, and understanding on your mission upon her.
- The air you breathe brings you new life-force that transforms the old and forms the new.
- Give thanks for your journey, honour your life as you honour the self.
- Ask for your new journey to be presented to you, ask to be placed upon your path of higher purpose.
- Spend time visualising leading the life you love.

Keep a journal and write down your thoughts and feelings.

This is an exercise that connects you with yourself and connects you with the world around you. Although we are not doing any visualisation, you will find that thoughts and feelings and dreams come to you. Let them come and go. Just write down what you are feeling.

There is time in the final step on the path to take your dreams and create what you want to create with them. Now it is about celebration and love.

Affirmation

↷ I am now free of all past constraints. I love leading the life I love.

ABUNDANCE

∞☙

How To Have Emotional Freedom And Let Your Spirit Soar

A LOVING HEART THAT APPRECIATES
ALL THINGS WILL DELIVER TO YOU
THE GIFT OF ABUNDANCE.

Freedom comes to you by living your life in a perfect way that suits you. Living life in its fullness, being your potential, making a difference and loving it. It is a high level to function on but it will set your heart free, where issues and problems are seldom.

Our planet is totally abundant.

Native traditions speak of the fact that we all share the same parents, Mother Earth, father Sky. We are all related. Think of what a mother would want for her child. She would want that child to be happy, whole, and complete. Mother Earth wants this for you.

For me, emotional freedom comes with my willingness to focus upon what I want and take inspired action towards my goals and dreams, knowing that the universe loves and supports me.

Emotional freedom comes to me through my ability to believe all is well and, if things don't quite go how I want them to, I learn from it, get focused, and stay on the path I want to walk and in the direction I want to go.

When you can see the beauty and the gifts you already have, you are abundant. The amount of what you have is irrelevant. Abundance is a feeling that comes from your heart. It is something that you create, not something that is bestowed upon you. Once you understand the difference you can create the abundance you truly want.

Understanding Abundance

> ABUNDANCE LIES IN YOUR ABILITY
> TO KNOW THAT ALL YOUR NEEDS
> ARE MET – NOW AND TOMORROW.

Abundance is to see the beauty of the planet you live on. Abundance is a feeling that comes through acknowledging all the good things in your life with total appreciation. Abundance is humanity, love, care, and compassion for oneself and others. It is where life becomes a gift of creativity and enjoyment, free from the constraints of your conditioning.

Abundance In Business

> YOUR SUCCESS IS INTERLINKED
> WITH THE SUCCESS OF ANOTHER
> FOR THEN YOU HAVE TRUE PROSPERITY.

Abundance in business is doing what you love and loving the development of what you do. Abundance is to love being of service, to assist another. It's the feeling that you are fulfilling your spiritual mission and purpose on the earth.

Abundance in business is sharing your gifts and talents with others so we can all have and understand abundance. Abundance in business is a new era of humanity based on creativity, community, and compassion for each other.

Competition, greed, and a general lack of care will not be sustainable in business.

Abundance v Lack

> ABUNDANCE IS A MINDSET.
> SO IS LACK.

If only I had ... there is no 'If only'! You have it all right now. Abundance is not an amount of something or acquiring something. Abundance is in your ability to think rich!

I have known and worked with so many people with material riches and yet they fail to see their abundance. They have been depressed, ill, low on inspiration and energy, and generally unable to reach a place of happiness and freedom.

You cannot buy a feeling, it comes from within you. The feeling comes only from your ability to be the enlightened one. The wise one that knows what the true meaning and richness of life is. The one that gives and receives love.

Abundance And The True Art Of Profit And Prosperity

WHERE THERE IS NO LOVE,

THERE IS NO ABUNDANCE.

WHERE THERE IS ABUNDANCE,

THERE IS PROSPERITY.

WHERE THERE IS MONEY AND NO LOVE,

THERE IS NO PROSPERITY OR ABUNDANCE.

Money alone is not prosperity. Profit is not just money. The true art of profit has to put people first. The true art of profit and prosperity is built on care, compassion, and the highest regard for yourself and others. Only then can we all become and experience the beauty of abundance.

The Power Of A Collective Consciousness

COMMUNITY - THE ART OF YOUR SUCCESS IS IN THE HEART OF EVERY ONE OF US.

Your success is interlinked with the success of another. You as a human being cannot survive alone, you need other human beings. When hearts make a connection with hearts, success is already synchronized and orchestrated.

Through the power of community and mutual respect for each other, you create a higher consciousness that births new ideas, sparks your inspiration, and enables you to benefit from the productivity that only a community of likeminded souls can produce.

So venture out, let people know who you are. You are no longer in denial of yourself, or your gifts and talents to speak your message, get your voice heard and be seen.

Creativity v Competition

THERE IS ROOM ON THIS PLANET FOR US ALL. WHY WASTE ENERGY COMPETING WHEN YOU ARE ALREADY A WINNER?

There is room on this planet for us all to be in our potential. There is no need for competition. To compete over another is fear-based energy created from the insecure self.

When you fully embrace the true self you can shine in your creative spiritual essence and let your 'spirit' shine. Competition has no power over you. There is no competition, no race to be won.

The beauty of creativity is that it is the spirit of who you are shining through and will allow you to honour your magnificent self. To be truly successful in your life and business you will have to let others see you the beauty of you! Then you will be a magnet of attraction on all levels. When you know your spirit, magic is all around you.

Wellness v Illness

THERE IS NO ILLNESS

UNLESS YOU CHOOSE ILLNESS.

Workplace stress, doubt, worry, or anxiety are all fear-based illnesses. When you open up to an abundant mind, body, and spirit you have freedom to think well, feel well, and fill your spirit with healthy doses of inspiration. Start to focus on general well-being and never go into the drama of your 'poor me' story.

Through your life lessons you have derived a sense of self that will serve you for the rest of your life. Honour your wisdom, believe in you, and show gratitude and appreciation that all your experiences are creating new understanding, enlightenment, and growth so you can move forwards, creating your dream.

Abundance In Life

ABUNDANCE IS THE GIFT YOU GIVE TO YOURSELF

You will need to reach an abundant feeling in all areas of your life if you want to be the designer of your own destiny. Abundance in life is to acknowledge all that life has to give to you and all that it has already given you.

The universe loves you. I am very clear on what makes me happy in my lifestyle. I desire a very close connection with Mother Earth, that is why living out in the country and spending most of my time there is so vital for me.

I love simplicity and freedom. I love to be time rich and spend each day with the people I love in places that I love. I adore my personal, professional, and spiritual empowerment. I love the evolution of my life.

Understanding what makes you happy and then loving creating it is abundance in all its forms.

Abundance In Relationships

SEE EVERY PERSON AS A GIFT THAT HELPS YOU FIND THE TRUTH OF YOURSELF AND YOUR PRESENT SITUATION.

You can never change someone else but you can change yourself. People are always a mirror for you to self-reflect.

Abundance in all your relationships comes to you when you see the positive aspects of a person and then focus on the kind of relationship you desire to have with them.

Changing your relationships means changing your relationship with the self. Self-acceptance and self-love will allow you to accept and love others more. The more you do this, the more you will have an abundance of love.

Love just is. It reaches out for the best in people and accepts nothing less. When you are in an abundant relationship with the self you become healthy, whole, and complete and you will attract the same kind of person you want inside your own sacred space.

Leap Into Leadership

LEADERSHIP SPEAKS OF SELF EXPRESSION. WHEN YOU LEAD YOU USE YOUR POTENTIAL TO EXPRESS WHO AND WHAT YOU ARE.

Leadership is you living your purpose and not hiding your potential. Leadership is you making a difference in the world and expressing who and what you are.

This is both empowering and productive. As you take the transformation into leadership, you may feel the need to change your appearance, attitude, or activities to fit the new you. Allow others to 'see' you and alter the way they perceive you. Offer your gifts to others who are in need of your talents.

Why You Need To Lead

> LEADERSHIP OPENS THE DOOR
> THAT YOU HAVE KEPT CLOSED.

Use the gift of giving yourself permission to lead. When you do, you become a catalyst for others to lead. You give them permission to be their unique authentic self. When you lead from the heart you inspire others. Your inspiration creates a vacuum of energy for them to want to achieve their potential and to receive the true prosperity of life.

You are now a leader and a catalyst of freedom, happiness, and love. You are an inspiration for others to follow, free of their myth of fear.

Why Everything Must Have A Purpose

> THERE IS REASON IN PURPOSE.
> THAT IS WHY YOU ARE HERE
> ON THIS PLANET.

Purpose has meaning. Meaning has value. To value something is to treasure it. You have a purpose. Your life has meaning and you are valuable. So treasure yourself. Having a purpose to all that you create increases your zest for living and unleashes your inner passion and desire. To act with a purpose is passion that ignites the fire in you and keeps your inspiration high so you keep moving in the direction you choose to walk.

The Road Is Wide Open And Clear

Put your foot on the gas and rev it up a gear.

Keeping checking for your myth of fear. It will return to hunt you now and again but it has no power over you.

Sustainable lifestyle and business equals caring and sharing of yourself and others. Your path of beauty requires you to SEE that life is wonderful and you are here to enjoy the journey.

Keep it simple - be happy, believe in your truth, love yourself, and love the life you lead. Any conflict you experience is always inner conflict with the self. Confusion is always your refusal to 'see' the truth.

You now have two paths: You can choose to go forth into this beautiful experience and walk a path of beauty; or you can choose to stay asleep to it all and remain forever in the myth of fear.

However fearful you are, your fear will not move until you move. Fear only dissolves when you walk out of the coldness and into the warmth of unconditional love by saying yes to your own self-created leadership. Then you open up to a magical world of opportunities.

How do I know this? I have walked some of it and experienced it. I still have lots to experience and to achieve but I love the path I am on.

You may have come to the end of this little book but actually it is the beginning of a whole new life for you - a life of happiness and freedom. Take a moment to appreciate now the beauty of you, your creative and spiritual power, and the potential that you hold.

You are truly blessed so do not waste a moment of it - LIVE.

Rite Of Passage

> MAY YOU ALWAYS WALK IN BEAUTY
> TO ACKNOWLEDGE AND TO USE
> THE GIFTS AND TALENTS
> THE CREATOR GAVE TO YOU.

Congratulations. You have won the lottery of life!

I wish you the best from my heart to your heart as you now let your truth guide you. Your truth will protect you, it does not matter what others think of you. You know your truth. When you honour yourself and your truth, you cannot be hurt. Your armour is now only your good intent, self-love, and love for others.

Keep looking in the direction you choose to walk and stay on your path of beauty.

Exercise

SHOW ME THE WAY

- ➢ Create a clean and clutter-free environment.
- ➢ Relax and place your mind into neutral, think nothing.
- ➢ Let all the good things in your life past, present, and future fill your mind space.
- ➢ Imagine all that you experience as positive experiences that allow you to transform into your potential.
- ➢ Imagine you taking the lead and creating the life you love.
- ➢ Let your imagination give you the feeling of love, security, and care.
- ➢ Feel your potential, know you are powerful.

In this space of clarity just ask yourself what is the next step in your empowered leadership. Listen to your higher self and take action with love. Keep walking! Keep serving. Keep receiving. And your blueprint is there to assist others.

We enter this planet with nothing but love and we leave the same way!

What you choose to do in between the two worlds of earth and heaven is in your heart and your hands to create. You have the power. Go ahead and use it this world needs you!

ೱೲ

Abundance

It has been my honour and pleasure to walk this journey with you.

Let me leave you with this final statement:

> You are your own Destiny.
> Your Destiny is not outside of you,
> it comes from the calling within you.
> The path is open for you to walk
> and to create the good in your life.

Affirmation

🖋 I honour my wisdom. It is my truth. I keep my wisdom alive through my willingness to share it with others.

🖋 I am blessed.

Blessings

Julie Anne Hart

ABOUT THE AUTHOR

Julie Anne Hart is an Empowered Leadership Coach and Intuitive Consultant. Julie Anne works with her own philosophy a unique blend of Ancient Wisdom, spirituality and therapeutic techniques to empower your Leadership of the self in your life or business.

She hosts a range of courses and programmes, retreats, and Medicine Lodge days. Discover more about Julie Anne Hart at:

www.JulieAnneHart.com

You can reach her by email at:

julie@julieannehart.com

INDEX

A

abundance . 99, 100, 101, 102, 105, 106
abundant leadership 95
action ... 56, 63, 66, 69, 79, 82, 85, 100, 110
affirmation..23, 33, 51, 74, 86, 98, 111

B

beautiful . 3, 11, 39, 60, 84, 85, 90, 91, 108
beauty.iii, 5, 6, 8, 9, 10, 20, 22, 28, 40, 44, 55, 61, 72, 74, 75, 77, 79, 80, 81, 82, 83, 84, 86, 90, 100, 102, 104, 108, 109
birthright 13, 90, 96
blame and shame 3, 43
blessed ... 8, 27, 38, 41, 69, 91, 109, 111
blueprint 79, 110
business 41, 57, 60, 65, 76, 78, 86, 90, 95, 101, 104, 108

C

childhood 5
clutter 110
co-dependent 5, 13, 44
competition 101, 103, 104
confusion.. 5, 9, 10, 44, 60, 67, 82
constraints 39, 98, 100
control 5, 6, 38, 40, 69
create. 9, 10, 14, 20, 40, 48, 50, 60, 61, 63, 75, 77, 78, 79, 86, 89, 91, 94, 95, 98, 100, 103, 107, 110
creativity..5, 11, 100, 101, 104

Index

D

denial ... 10, 13, 16, 29, 43, 103
Divine love 12, 30, 89

E

empowerment.. 12, 16, 21, 36, 49, 50, 55, 56, 58, 60, 61, 62, 63, 65, 67, 70, 71, 73, 77, 83, 90, 105
energy 8, 11, 12, 14, 20, 33, 36, 37, 42, 60, 69, 70, 71, 75, 76, 80, 81, 82, 91, 92, 93, 97, 102, 103, 104, 107

F

false belief system 10, 15
fear based behaviours 69
freedom .. 9, 18, 21, 26, 27, 28, 29, 31, 43, 44, 46, 62, 77, 81, 100, 102, 104, 105, 107, 109

G

gifts 6, 8, 14, 27, 39, 78, 91, 93, 95, 100, 101, 103, 107, 109
greed 101

H

happiness 12, 84, 85, 89, 96, 102, 107, 109
harmony 12, 21, 50, 89
healthy 36, 60, 104, 106
hunt 108
hurt 32, 109

I

impatience 69
indecisiveness 68, 83
intuition. 49, 60, 68, 71, 73, 80, 84, 94
intuitive 21, 73

J

journey 3, 9, 10, 12, 21, 26, 31, 33, 35, 36, 38, 42, 56, 61, 63, 65, 66, 67, 69, 71, 73, 76, 78, 90, 92, 94, 97, 108, 111

L

learning 4, 43, 93
lifestyle 83, 90, 105, 108
lovable 16, 92

M

Macdonald, Susan 8
Medicine Woman 8
mentor 48, 68, 71, 72

O

opportunities ... 11, 18, 21, 29, 60, 71, 92, 94, 108

P

painful 5, 13, 14, 27, 38, 46, 48, 51
parents ... 5, 30, 35, 36, 40, 41, 42, 44, 47, 99
passion . 15, 20, 56, 60, 64, 77, 80, 91, 97, 107
past. 11, 15, 16, 17, 18, 20, 29, 30, 31, 33, 41, 48, 61, 92, 98, 110
perfect.... 4, 14, 41, 43, 47, 86, 99
playfulness 4
positive... 5, 11, 12, 14, 18, 36, 37, 41, 42, 43, 59, 70, 71, 80, 81, 91, 106, 110
potential..... 4, 5, 6, 10, 11, 12, 13, 14, 15, 21, 27, 28, 29, 31, 37, 43, 55, 56, 57, 60, 65, 70, 71, 73, 75, 77, 78, 79, 80, 82, 84, 85, 86, 89, 90, 93, 96, 99, 104, 106, 107, 109, 110
power ... 4, 6, 9, 10, 13, 14, 16, 17, 18, 26, 27, 29, 31, 33, 39, 41, 42, 44, 46, 47, 49, 56, 59, 68, 69, 76, 80, 81, 83, 85, 86, 89, 94, 95, 96, 103, 104, 108, 109, 110
practice listening 68
psyche 4
purpose .. 4, 15, 16, 17, 18, 29, 37, 40, 77, 78, 85, 89, 93, 95, 96, 97, 101, 106, 107

R

receive.. 10, 14, 20, 31, 39, 47, 49, 57, 58, 61, 64, 66, 69, 80, 85, 86, 89, 90, 92, 93, 94, 96, 107
relationships. 6, 13, 35, 36, 39, 40, 41, 43, 50, 60, 65, 70, 105, 106
resistance 69
responsibility 3, 30, 44, 62, 63, 64, 72

S

sabotage 69
sacred space 47, 73, 106
sadness 4, 96
self-love 106, 109

Index

self-reflect 106
sense of self 5, 23, 104
solar plexus 73, 94
soul 14, 67, 75
spirituality 8

T

talents 6, 13, 14, 36, 73, 91, 93, 95, 101, 103, 107, 109
traditions 99
transformation. 3, 7, 16, 21, 30, 36, 43, 44, 64, 72, 80, 106
transition 13, 25
truth 3, 5, 6, 7, 9, 10, 11, 13, 14, 16, 17, 18, 19, 21, 22, 28, 29, 36, 37, 38, 40, 41, 42, 44, 45, 47, 48, 51, 62, 65, 75, 76, 78, 80, 81, 83, 84, 93, 95, 105, 108, 109, 111

U

unconditional love .. 11, 27, 28, 30, 45, 108

V

vacuum 107
vision 3, 7, 77, 80, 86, 94
visualisation 98

W

whole 4, 18, 19, 29, 43, 50, 64, 78, 82, 85, 99, 106, 109
wisdom .. 15, 18, 21, 23, 42, 46, 60, 67, 73, 77, 82, 91, 93, 104, 111

Z

zest 107

Printed in Great Britain
by Amazon